Hats & Helmets

Written by

**Dawn Daffinee, CPM®, and
Kelly Blaskowsky, CPM®**

Order this book online at www.trafford.com
or email orders@trafford.com

Most Trafford titles are also available at major online book retailers.

The stories in this book are used to illustrate stories that have occurred in our day-
to-day lives managing real estate. No real names have been used. The author and
publisher disclaims all responsibility for any liability of the contents of this book.

Print information available on the last page.

ISBN: 978-1-4907-5657-8 (sc)
ISBN: 978-1-4907-5658-5 (hc)
ISBN: 978-1-4907-5656-1 (e)

Library of Congress Control Number: 2015903886

Trafford rev. 03/11/2015

 www.trafford.com

North America & international
toll-free: 1 888 232 4444 (USA & Canada)
fax: 812 355 4082

I dedicate this book to my amazing daughter Jennifer
and wonderful son Jason for all of their support during
this new adventure. They are truly my inspiration.

- Dawn Daffinee, CPM®

I would like to dedicate this book to my wonderful husband
Keith and my two beautiful daughters Ariel and Amber for
their patience and valued input. They are the light of my life.

- Kelly Blaskowsky, CPM®

Preface

My name is Dawn Daffinee, CPM®, and I am the New Jersey Portfolio Real Estate Manager for a company headquartered in New York. A wonderful friend, Kelly Blaskowsky, CPM®, and I decided to write a book together. We have a common goal to write our book. She would write on her experiences as a property manager on the residential/multifamily side, and I would write on my experiences on the commercial side. We set out on our journey together in hopes that we can inspire other property managers by telling our stories of what we do in our property management profession.

At the time, we were not sure what we were getting ourselves into. We just wanted to share our experiences with others. In the past, others would ask me how I got into property management. Just recently, an assistant property manager working in the residential field of management asked me how I got into commercial real estate management. Of course I helped her, and if we can help others understand what we do and inspire others to become real estate managers, then I know I needed to write this book with Kelly.

I have been in property management for over twenty-five years. I love what I do each and every day. Being a property manager means wearing many hats, with each day being something different. I am a certified property manager (CPM®) through the Institute of Real Estate Management (IREM) since 1992. I have held a Texas and New Jersey real estate license since 1988 and have loved working in the real estate field. In addition, I obtained my bachelor's degree in management and received an MBA in 2002. I'm an active participant in the Institute of Real Estate Management organization and have served in several national positions as a volunteer to assist in educating up-and-coming real estate professionals. My positions that I am most proud of with IREM have been those that have allowed me to serve a large body of members and continue to promote the education and ethics that IREM provides. I've served as the president of the San Antonio chapter in 2011, regional vice president over seven chapters spread throughout Texas and Oklahoma, as well as my recent nomination and election to the board of directors of the IREM Foundation for a three-year term.

For those who may not know what I do as a property manager, I will, in our book, reflect on some of the things I do to ensure the assets are profitable and well maintained. I have managed class-A office buildings, medical buildings, high-rises, retail strip centers, shopping centers, land properties, and other types of real estate over the years. My goal and ambition is to share my passion for management and the organizations that can provide continuing education.

My name is Kelly Blaskowsky, CPM® and I am a Vice President in the multi-family industry. I hold a certificate through the Texas Apartment Association as a certified apartment manager as well as through IREM as a certified property manager. I have been in many positions while working in the multifamily industry, including but not limited to leasing agent, leasing director, assistant manager, floating manager, manager, district manager, and so on. Each position has taught me great lessons and helped me groom my own management style by taking nuggets of information from each supervisor I have worked with. I have worked on all types of assets, both class A and class F (if that can really be defined). My expertise is with affordable properties, those that have federal funding or state funding of some sort, due to the number of years I have worked with that particular type of portfolio. I began my career as a part-time leasing agent on a class-B property with 320 units on two phases. I started this job in conjunction with a waitressing job I worked at night to make ends meet. My next step was to move to Austin, Texas, and I took a job as a full-time leasing agent making $9 per hour, which was more than I had ever made thus far, and was thrilled to take it. The property was filled primarily with students, and I enjoyed the fast-paced environment. The company I worked for noticed my enjoyment of the pace and offered me a leasing director position at a brand-new community. I jumped at the opportunity and welcomed the challenge.

The lease-up was a great success; in a year, we had full occupancy and began to look and feel like a stabilized asset. We made yet another move to San Antonio, Texas, where I found a job with an alternate company as an assistant manager in a two-person office on a class-B property. This step was an important step for me. Within two years, I went from an assistant manager to a floating manager to assist, to a manager, and then a manager over two properties. The job was great, and I enjoyed the position I'd been given, but alas, there was a greater opportunity that was presented for more money to open a class-A new construction property. I took the opportunity and, within one year, was transferred to a larger class-B property in Fort Worth, Texas. This was my first touch with an affordable program. I realized fairly quickly that the affordability component translated to more paperwork and a challenged clientele. Within another year, I successfully occupied and stabilized the property and was promoted again to assistant district manager. This job encompassed supervising a portfolio of four to five properties, which were made up of conventional, affordable, and one HUD property. I gained a wealth of knowledge and experience working with the assets and their teams and, once again, was promoted to a district manager with a portfolio of 1800 units or eight properties. I remained in the Dallas/Fort Worth, Texas, area for approximately three years before I was asked to transfer to Phoenix, Arizona, to manage an alternate portfolio. I accepted the offer and remained in Phoenix for two years before finally moving back to San

Antonio, Texas. In San Antonio, I accepted an offer for a regional manager position for a company that had a projected growth of eight to ten assets each year. Six years later, the company has gone from four thousand units to thirteen thousand units, and I am managing a portfolio of fifty-two properties, or seven thousand units with five regional managers. I love what I do and only hope that each person I meet can take a nugget of information to assist them in their growth when they leave.

I am writing this book in conjunction with a fellow property manager and my very good friend, Dawn Daffinee. I met Dawn through IREM in San Antonio, and although we both work in property management, our worlds are very different, and I love comparing and talking about the differences with her. Although the environment may be different, the basics of property management are the same, and I am thrilled for the opportunity to write this together and share our experiences with you.

The Hat of Listening and Problem Solving
Dawn Daffinee, CPM®

M y first office building was thirteen stories high and lined with mirrors and glass. The entire building was 206,000 square feet separated into various sizes of office space and considered a class-A office building due to the number of luxuries we offered. The entryway was lined with plants in various shades of green with a small sitting area in between the two hallways of elevators. I had never managed a building as a property manager, and being given this opportunity to work for a national real estate company was absolutely mind-blowing. It was an exciting opportunity, and I was full of enthusiasm for what each day held.

One day in particular that I will never forget was my first day on the job. As I walked through the lobby, my heels on the cold marble floor had a ring of enthusiasm and almost sounded as if I was skipping. I took the elevator up to the tenth floor and was welcomed by my receptionist. "Welcome to the Vantage. How can I help you?"

I was so excited, I didn't know where to start. "Hi, I am the new property manager," I said confidently.

"Oh, I am so happy to meet you. My name is Susan, and I am your receptionist. We are all so happy to have you here. Please, let me show you to your office, and I will introduce you to the staff once you get settled."

I smiled and followed her down the hallway, nodding at a couple of people on the way. We came to a set of dark wooden double doors with dark brown wood trim. Susan slowly pushed open the heavy wooden doors, and I could almost hear the music. *Ah . . . It felt like a dream.* There in front of me was a wall of windows from floor to ceiling, showing off a gorgeous view of San Antonio. As my eyes swept across the room, there was a large green plant in the corner near the door and a large heavy wooden desk trimmed in ornate design, accompanied by a large credenza with the same detailed design as the desk. To the right of the room sat a tall bookshelf filled with binders and a few leadership books (good ones, I might add) and a multifunctional copier/printer on a smaller wood table. This office was absolutely amazing, and I felt utterly speechless.

"Well, I'll come by later to check on you. Your calendar is on the desk along with your log-in sheets to get you started. See you soon," Susan said as she begins to exit the office.

"Thank you, Susan. I'm excited to be here," I said, smiling at her.

Later that afternoon, Susan introduced me to Becky, the accountant; David, my property assistant; and Brett and Mark, the building engineers. The entire team was incredibly welcoming, and I had a few minutes with each person to get to know them a bit. This was going to be the best job ever. Have you heard the saying "spoke too soon"? Well, that saying proved to be quite accurate today.

One of our more assertive tenants stormed past Susan, the receptionist, and blew past David, my assistant, and all the way to the back of the office until he reached my office.

"Are you the new property manager?" the tenant stated with a bright red face and an intensity that felt like he was going to burst.

"Yes, my name is Dawn. How can I help you?" I said with the biggest smile I could muster.

The tenant stopped and took in a deep breath. He was a tall slender man with dark black hair and green eyes. He was obviously a doctor since he was still wearing his badge and white coat. His badge read "Dr. Fennel." I could tell he was mad at something but wasn't sure how quickly I could diffuse the situation since I wasn't familiar with the building yet.

"I am so glad the other lady is gone. She was worthless! I've been a tenant here for over three years, and for the last six months, I've reported several thefts from my office. First, it was just small items like large bags of cotton swabs and alcohol packages. Then they began taking smaller equipment like a blood pressure monitor and thermometers, but today is the final straw! I'm now missing one of the front-desk computers!"

Dr. Fennel was quickly rattling through a rapid firing of obscenities. He was heated! I let him continue with his concerns and realized quickly that the best thing to do now would be to stop and just listen. I did not have the answers, and from what I could tell, Dr. Fennel really just needed to report his frustrations. Apparently, the manager before me had been informed about the theft but, according to Dr. Fennel, did nothing about it.

After listening to every detail of Dr. Fennel's concerns, I gave a quick nod and wrote down a few notes for myself. "Dr. Fennel, I do apologize that you've had a bad experience, however, I'm here now and am more than happy to look into this further and will get back to you as soon as I have a chance to gather some information. It's my first day today, and I am not familiar with your particular situation, but I will get up to speed quickly."

Dr. Fennel stared at me with fire in his eyes and said, "Well, you'd better! I will not be ignored anymore!" With that, he walked out of my office and straight past my team.

"Holy cow!" I thought. *"What in the world did I get into with this new job?"* I took a few minutes to get my thoughts together and grabbed a pen and paper. I pressed the intercom button on my desk phone and said, "David, would you mind coming in for a moment?"

"Sure thing, Dawn," David replied.

David walked in a couple of minutes later with a pad and pen in his hand. He immediately took a seat across from me at the desk.

"Thanks for coming in, David. I just spoke with Dr. Fennel, and he was pretty upset about a recent theft in his office. Are you familiar with his situation?"

David sighed and stated, "I'm very familiar with Dr. Fennel and have received several complaints from other tenants about missing supplies. We've reported it to our security company, but the problem just seems to be getting worse. The last property manager was in communication with all the tenants about the theft and was keeping a log but never seemed to get anywhere, which is why Dr. Fennel is so upset. I figured something else had come up missing when he stormed in. He's usually very pleasant."

"Where are the incident reports with the details of each theft?" I asked.

David stood up and walked over to the bookshelf and pulled out a large black binder. "Everything you need is in here."

"Thank you, David. I'll dig through this and call you if I need you."

"No problem," David said as he exited the office.

I read through each incident in the binder and pulled up the security reports to review and compare to the incidents. What I found proved to be very interesting. I noticed the security company's name was VA Security. The name itself wasn't interesting; however, the janitorial company was also mentioned in the incident reports, and their name was VA Janitorial. That was interesting. Could they be the same company? Or could it be a really strange coincidence?

I called the security company and asked for the general manager, Don. I introduced myself and quickly began my line of questioning. "Could you tell me a little bit about the theft history?"

Don replied, "Well, I tried telling the previous manager, but hopefully, you will listen. We've been investigating the incidents reported by the tenants and have noticed that the janitorial company is typically the last people in the office when the items go missing."

"Have you questioned the janitorial staff to see if you can determine who is taking the items?" I asked.

"Yes, we've talked to Debbie, and she says it isn't her team. I even showed her the reports from my officer and gave her the names of the people we think it might be, but I don't think she's taken it any further," Don stated.

"Thank you for the information, Don. I'm going to continue to look into this and get back to you," I said as I ended our call. The information I received from Don seemed to make sense, and I felt my only logical step was to call Debbie at the janitorial company.

I called VA Janitorial and asked for Debbie. Debbie was extremely friendly and offered the same information I heard from Don, except she felt it was the security officers stealing the items and quickly dismissed any accusations directed toward her team. She insisted that Don was covering for them and knew her story to be true. I hung up with Debbie and felt more confused than ever. I pulled up the vendor file and reviewed both the security and janitorial company ownerships. That was still bothering me, and I had to get to the bottom of it.

What do I find . . . ? The janitorial and security companies were in fact under the same ownership! I couldn't believe my eyes: what were the odds that both companies would be owned by the same person? Something just did not feel right . . .
The hat of problem solving was kicking in.

Being the "new" kid on the block, I knew in order to win over my first assertive tenant, I had to solve this problem . . . and fast. I couldn't believe how long this had been going on, and I had a pretty good idea of what I could do to eliminate this issue.

I decided to search for other security companies and provided each potential replacement security company with a full scope of services that we expected to receive. A beautiful building like this could not allow such an activity to continue, and finding the right company to watch over our tenants' assets was my first priority. It took a couple of days to obtain all the bids, but it was worth the wait to ensure I was choosing the right company. Once I received all three bids from the potential security companies, I reviewed and chose what I felt was the best security option for the budget we had. I immediately provided a thirty-day notice to VA Security and knew I was doing the right thing.

Don called—which I expected—and was upset about the changes, claiming that we were unjustified in the notice and began listing the benefits he felt they offered. I quickly cut him off and apologized for his dissatisfaction with my decision; however, my decision stood and would continue with the thirty-day notice. Don made a rash decision to pull off from the property immediately and waived the thirty-day notice. I agreed and contacted our new company to begin immediately. This issue was now considered closed. It did not stop my theft problem, but I felt I was one step closer.

My next step was to remove and replace the janitorial company. If the security company blamed the janitorial and vice versa, then the best thing to do was to get rid of them both. I set out to begin collecting bids for janitorial service. I'm assuming Debbie got wind of my search since I received a call from her shortly after I submitted for bids.

"Hi, Dawn," said Debbie. "I heard you were looking for another janitorial company. Can I ask why?"
I was completely taken off guard but had to be ready for situations like this. "Hi, Debbie," I said. "Yes, we are receiving bids on janitorial service. As you are aware, we've had several incidents in the last six months and have decided to switch up a few things."

"Well, I told you who was doing it. Have you talked to Don?" Debbie said with a hint of frustration.
"Yes, I've spoken with Don, and we've already switched security companies, and the problem still exists. I'm not blaming anyone, but am switching things around in the best interest of my tenants," I stated as professionally as I could.
Debbie stayed silent for a moment before taking a deep breath of what sounded like defeat and stated, "I understand. When should we expect the thirty-day notice?"

I wasn't quite prepared for this response, but when in Rome . . .

"We will be sending that out to you today," I said, hoping that I could round up a janitorial service quickly.

"Thank you," Debbie stated as she hung up the phone.

Phew, I thought as I hung up and sat back in my still soft and supple desk chair. *That went a little better than I thought*, I said to myself.

Over the next week, the janitorial company ended their services almost immediately, and I had a new company who was providing excellent service. The new vendors I'd brought in were operating beautifully, and best of all, the theft had stopped almost as soon as both companies were gone. I had conquered my first challenge and felt *fantastic*!

I went by Dr. Fennel's office in hopes of hearing good news and/or catching him on a good day. I walked into a waiting room with a small window framing a stern woman who was fully engrossed in her work. I walked up to the small window and asked for Dr. Fennel and left her my name. I turned around and sat on one of the small orange chairs with wood trim and began sorting through the various magazines on a wide brown coffee table. I was only there for a couple of minutes when a nurse came through the back door and said, "Dawn Daffinee, the doctor will see you now." I looked up and smiled as I rose to follow her into the back offices. The doctor's patients who were waiting in the room glared at me as if I had just cut in line. *Ouch*, I thought. I wished I could explain, but no chance now.

I followed the nurse through the hallway to an office in the back. The hallway was your typical doctor's office with photos of farms and flowers on the wall. The smell of freshly pumped sanitizer filled the air. As we approached the back office, I could see the nameplate on the outside of the door, "Dr. Fennel," and swallowed the lump in my throat. *Stay strong*, I told myself. I wasn't sure what kind of welcome I was going to receive and hadn't heard of any further incidents, so I was hopeful.

I entered Dr. Fennel's office and said, "Hi, Dr. Fennel. I just wanted to check in with you and see how things are going." I stated this with a timid smile on my face.

Dr. Fennel stood and held out his arms with a big smile on his face and stated, "Dawn, so good to see you! Thank you so much for listening to me the other day. I've noticed you've made a few changes, and those changes must have worked because I haven't had anything come up missing since. Thank you for taking care of that issue for us. I can't tell you how much that means to us."

"I'm so happy to hear that. We are just happy you're feeling better about your choice in office space. I'd like you to remain here as long as possible," I replied with a now full-blown smile.

Dr. Fennel and I became great friends after that. There was a level of trust he had in me as his property manager to get the job done, and I was glad to be doing it. From that day forward, every time I ran into Dr. Fennel in the elevator, he would drop various hard candies into my purse with a smile and give me a friendly greeting. I knew I made a tenant very happy.

Having a bachelor's degree in management or an MBA did not prepare me for something like this. I never thought my first day on the job as a property manager would be so rough. However, I learned quickly that to be a good property manager, you have to be a good listener first and foremost.

I mentioned at the beginning that property managers wear many hats . . .

This time, the hat of listening really helped.

The Helmet of Problem Solving
Kelly Blaskowsky, CPM®

At the time, I managed a large three-hundred-unit property with a team of nine employees. The property was approximately four years old and had all the luxuries one could ask for. The entry contained a large clubroom divided in two, with one side housing a large pool table and the other a set of sofas with a 55-inch TV that can be seen from both sides of the clubroom that connected to a fully furnished leasing center with two offices and a large workroom in the back. To the right was a large hallway that took you directly to a fully loaded fitness center with large picture windows that faced the pool for a spectacular view and two 32-inch TVs mounted to the wall in case you wanted to catch up on a few TV shows. On the other side of the hallway was a state-of-the-art business center with six top-of-the-line computers set in private cubbies made of stained dark wood coupled with smooth beige leather desk chairs and a large printer/scanner in the back. As you exit to the back of the office, you walk out onto a large patio with three sets of tables and chairs and a gate that entered into the pool area. The pool area was surrounded with lounge chairs and a few tables with umbrellas for additional seating. There were two playground areas with large play sets and slides surrounded by small rubber chips for a soft landing. The property was large and full of amenities, but as all property managers know, it also means plenty of hours in maintenance to keep everything fully functional and clean.

The day was like any other day with phones ringing; people coming in, being served by one of the associates; and emails floating in like dripping water (every few seconds). Today was report day, so my mind and energy were focused on completing my reports before the end of the day. My team was excellent about attempting to solve any resident concerns during days like these, but today I was not so lucky. As I'm sitting in my office, adding up the invoices I have on my desk, I hear voices beginning to slightly raise. I lay down my pen for a moment to determine if what I hear could be a problem before I see Debbie, the leasing consultant, walking swiftly toward my office. She opens the door and, with a panicked look in her eyes, says, "I need your help. Ms. Dozier is in the office, and she is extremely upset but doesn't want to talk to me. I tried calming her down, but she started yelling, so I came to get you."

This was obviously something that required immediate attention, and I rose from my desk saying, "No problem. I'll come out and bring her back to my office. Thank you, Debbie."
As I entered the leasing center, Ms. Dozier is glaring at us with a look of impatience and is visibly upset. "Good morning, Ms. Dozier," I say, extending my hand in a greeting style to hopefully defuse some of her anger.

"Susie," she says, "I need to speak with you about my neighbor. I've had enough of her and need you to do something about it."

"Let's head back to my office," I say, "and discuss this further to see how I can help you."

We walk to my office, and I offer her a seat in front of my desk. As she sits, she immediately begins spilling all her frustration and anger.

"I am so sick of having to deal with this type of treatment from my neighbor. I pay good money to live here and have a full-time job, so why should I have to put up with this? I need you to evict that woman out of the property. She shouldn't be here, and I know for a fact she has people coming over at night with drugs so they can party. So what are you going to do about it?"

It was so much information at one time; it was difficult for me to determine exactly what the complaint was. I spoke as evenly and calmly as possible, "What exactly happened that brought you in here today, and how can I help to resolve it?"

Ms. Dozier takes a deep breath and says, "Well, last night I came home late from work, and the neighbor was parked in my parking spot. I pay for that spot so when I work late I don't have to look for parking, and this wasn't the first time she'd parked there. I went to her apartment and knocked on her door to ask her to move her car, and she had the nerve to slam the door in my face. I called the office, and the answering service said they would call you, but I never heard from you and ended up parking two buildings over. That's a long way for me to walk by myself in the dark. She knows that's my parking space. Don't you guys tow the cars when they do that? Can I have her car towed?"

"Ms. Dozier," I say, "I can certainly see why you're upset and will address this immediately with your neighbor. We have you assigned to that space, and I am sure we can resolve this for you."

Ms. Dozier was still angry and quickly stated, "Well, I guess so, but you may want to check her apartment too. I'm pretty sure you'll find drugs."

"Thank you, Ms. Dozier. I will follow up with it." I walk her out of the office and shake her hand good-bye. When I get back to my desk, I immediately research her neighbor, Ms. Angleton, to find her contact information to give her a quick call. That seems to be the most logical approach to resolving the situation. I locate the information and begin dialing her number. It rings twice before a young woman answers, "Hello."

"Hello, my name is Susie Major, the property manager at Sunnyside Apartments. Is Ms. Angleton available?"

"This is she," states Ms. Angleton.

"Hi, Ms. Angleton. I have a small concern I'd like to speak with you about if you have time."

Ms. Angleton pauses before stating, "How can I help you?"

"There's a concern that's been brought to our attention regarding a parking situation. It appears that last night you parked in an assigned parking space that inevitably caused a neighbor to have to park a couple of buildings away even though she pays for the spot. If you're interested in a parking space, we do have one in the same area we can lease to you."

Ms. Angleton immediately begins yelling. "I can't believe she went into the office. Listen, what you don't know is that Lexi [Ms. Dozier] has been harassing me for days. I didn't park in her spot or even talk to her. I don't know what her problem is, but I didn't do anything wrong. If anything, you need to talk *to her.*"

Not exactly what I was expecting to hear. Any time you have two conflicting stories, who's to say which one is correct? I'm not a mind reader by any stretch of the imagination, but I was now realizing that this was not going to be an easy fix. "How has Ms. Dozier been harassing you? Have you reported it to our office?" I responded.

Ms. Angleton takes a deep breath and says in a defeated tone, "Just forget about it. There is nothing you can do, and she will probably stop. I didn't park in her spot, so I'm not sure what to tell you about that. It was probably someone else with a car like mine. Anyway, if there's nothing else, I have a ton of things to do."

I realize that this was a quick ending after all and stated, "Thank you, Ms. Angleton, and please feel free to contact me if there are any concerns." Once I hung up with Ms. Angleton, I pulled out both files and documented the conversations, just in case the situation came up again.

A couple of days went by with no word regarding the parking situation, and I figured it was taken care of. The main focus of the day was the preparation for a resident party we had planned for later that afternoon. The day was cooperating nicely with a slight breeze, and the sun was shining bright. Just breezy enough to wear a sweater or light jacket, and the property was buzzing with excitement and preparation. The pool area was being power washed by the maintenance team while Debbie and I were making a list of what was needed from the grocery store. Lynn, the assistant manager, was holding down the office phone calls and walk-in visitors with Sandra's help (leasing professional). The party was scheduled from 4:00 p.m. to 6:00 p.m., and I had planned on serving hot dogs with all the fixings, chips, and soda. All we needed was the hot dogs and buns, so the trip should be quick and easy.

I left the office feeling fantastic and anxious to get the party going. We were planning on feeding one hundred people but expected at least fifty, which was pretty good because most resident parties have ten or less people actually showing up. This particular party was our annual pool party, which historically has always proven to be a favorite. Free food and a DJ always did the trick.

When I arrived back from the store, I entered the clubroom through the side door and heard a large commotion coming from the pool area. I set the bags of food down on the clubroom kitchen counter and walked out to the pool area to see what was going on. When I arrived at the pool, I came upon Ms. Angleton, Ms. Dozier, and Debbie talking rather loudly, and it looked as if Debbie was attempting to calm the two women down. Ms. Angleton looked like she was in her thirties and always appeared neatly dressed in a suit and conservative heels with her hair pulled back in a bun. Ms. Dozier appeared to be in her late twenties but much more relaxed in her attire with baggy jeans, a loose blouse, and flip-flops. Her hair was always in a messy ponytail, and she rarely wore makeup. The two were polar opposites of one another; no wonder they didn't get along. I walked swiftly over to Debbie and the two ladies as Debbie looked at me with an expression of relief. She hated dealing with conflict, so I assumed my timing was perfect.

"Ladies, please calm down. Can someone please calmly explain to me what's happened?"
Debbie spoke up instantly, "I was setting up the decorations when Ms. Dozier walked by and offered to help. I accepted her help since there was so much left to do and figured we could be done quicker with the extra set of hands. So Ms. Dozier began putting the streamers on the gate when Ms. Angleton arrived in the parking lot and saw Ms. Dozier at the pool. Ms. Angleton walked over here and asked Ms. Dozier why she was lying to us and—"

"That's not exactly how it happened," interrupted Ms. Angleton. "When I got out of my car, I looked over at the pool, and Lexi was staring at me. When I caught her eye, she threw me the finger, so I walked up to confront her."
"Ms. Angleton," I say, "I think it would be better if you came into my office with me so we can—"

"This is crap!" yells Ms. Angleton. "I've had enough of you taking sides with her. You don't even know what's really going on. I'm out of here." Ms. Angleton angrily stomps away back to her apartment.

I look at Ms. Dozier and say, "I'm not sure what is going on, but it would be best if you and Ms. Angleton do not speak to one another." Ms. Dozier just nods and goes back to placing the decorations alongside Debbie. I head back into the office, hoping that this is the end, but I know that it's not over yet.

The party was a huge success. I didn't count the number of people but went through 150 hot dogs and ran out of sodas and chips by the time 6:00 p.m. rolled around. My team did a great job serving the food and helping the residents with finding seats and directing them to the facilities. We all left work a little late that night but were pleased when a couple of residents stayed behind to help clean up. The next morning, the office was ready for business, and all of us were happy to have the party behind us since there were other projects we could now focus on. I strolled over to the copy room and took the papers off the fax machine to review the answering-service messages as I do every morning. The first call I see is from Ms. Angleton.

"Here we go again," I say to no one in particular. The message reads:

To: Susie—Manager
From: Sarah Angleton

Message: Susie, this is Ms. Angleton, and I am calling to let you know that Lexi came to my apartment again tonight and kept banging on my door, yelling obscenities. I already called the police but wanted to report it to you. If you want to call me back, my number is 555-567-5099.

As I read the message, I thought through the timeline of events and what action we had already taken versus what options we had today. In addition, I pulled the communication logs I recorded earlier to review what was written in an effort to determine the reason these two particular residents were fighting and possibly resolve it or try to, at least. I wasn't interested in making them friends, just calming them enough to allow each other to live comfortably. The one thing we all forget as property managers in multifamily is that even though where we are is work for us—to our residents, it is their home. It's the place where they are raising their children, spending their holidays, and enjoying quality time with one another.

As I thought back to my initial conversation with Ms. Dozier, I remembered her mentioning Ms. Angleton's evening parties and potential drugs, which anyone who knew Ms. Angleton or saw her would think was an absolutely false accusation. My conversation with Ms. Angleton was not as direct, and she seemed to give up quickly even though she was adamant Ms. Dozier was lying about the parking incident and even indicated she had been harassing her prior to this incident. I decided it was time to bring both women in and have a discussion together. I wasn't fond of this method as it can very quickly go from bad to worse, so it is smart to have plenty of staff members around as witnesses or possible assistants. However, with the situation continuing to escalate, I felt it was important to work through to avoid any further incidents. I contacted both Ms. Dozier and Ms. Angleton that afternoon and made an appointment to meet them first thing in the morning. Both were agreeable and seemed to have the same desire I did—to put an end to it.

The next morning, I opened up the office as the team slowly rolled in and prepared for the day. My first objective of the morning was the "meeting." I dreaded it but was also anxious to get it over with. There was a small table and chairs to the side of the clubroom I had intended on conducting the meeting. I preferred it to be in the common area for two reasons: one, to create a feeling of "public" so that the residents did not become comfortable enough to begin yelling, and two, to ensure the team could hear the discussions and/or read the body language to intervene if necessary. The last time I had a meeting between two residents in my office, the yelling began; and let's just say ten minutes later, the cops are there making an arrest for assault, and the other resident is walking away with ice on his eye. The discussion escalated so quickly to aggression, I didn't have time to flag anyone to come in, and no one heard the argument until it was too late. I wouldn't make that mistake again.

A few minutes later, Ms. Dozier walks through the door. She's in her typical baggy jeans and loose blouse with flip-flops; but this morning, her hair is fixed nicely, and she has just a touch of eyeliner and gloss that made her look fresh and lively. I showed her to the table where we were going to meet and offered her a cup of coffee. As I'm pouring the cup of coffee, in walks Ms. Angleton. She's calm but has a stern look to her. She's in fitted jeans and a T-shirt. Not the normal look for her, but still well put together as usual. I greet Ms. Angleton and offer her a cup of coffee as well. She declines, and I walk her to the table with Ms. Dozier's cup of coffee in my hands. I set the mug of coffee down and immediately sit to begin the meeting before they have a chance to talk.

"Thank you both for coming in," I say. "I've heard from both of you and was hoping that the situation at hand would correct itself, but there appears to be quite a bit happening after hours that is making this situation worse. I'd like to resolve this for both of you, but I need your help to come to a reasonable solution. I'd also like to set some ground rules for this discussion to keep us all calm and comfortable."

Both women looked at each other with a scowl and then looked back at me with the same scowl. I was sure they were going to disagree and interrupt, but both women appeared to be willing, so I continued.

"Rule 1: No interruptions while someone is talking. It's important we hear everything the other has to say. Rule 2: No standing or shouting. If you feel as if your emotions are becoming too much to handle, please remove yourself from the table to cool off before speaking. Rule 3: After we come to a resolution, I expect both of you to live with the agreement you've made to allow the other to live comfortably. Any questions?"

Both women nodded slightly in agreement. I handed them both a piece of paper and had them sign in acknowledgment to the rules I just provided. I knew that the document was nothing more than a piece of paper, but I utilized it as a tool to hold them accountable for anything we agreed to.

"Let's begin," I say. "Ms. Dozier, you've indicated three things that you have concerns with, and I would like for you to please confirm. You've indicated that Ms. Angleton has parked in your assigned parking space, that she is having parties at night, and that you have approached her before with no resolution. Correct?"
Ms. Dozier looks at Ms. Angleton and states firmly, "Correct."
"Ms. Angleton, you've indicated two items as well. That Ms. Dozier has a history of harassing you, that you did not park in the assigned parking and had not spoken with Ms. Dozier. Is that correct?"
Ms. Angleton looks down at the table and states, "That's correct."

"From what I can tell," I began, "both of you seem to have the stories wrong, but obviously have a problem with one another. Is there something more that's happening that would have created this animosity between the two of you?"

Both women sigh and look away from me and each other. I stay quiet to see if either will speak up first, and seconds before I start the next question, Ms. Dozier speaks up and says with a sigh, "I'm sorry. This is my fault. Sarah and I don't know each other, but she just started dating my ex-boyfriend. I've been mad at her because she knows he was with me, yet she parades him around like she is trying to make me jealous."

Well, this was a *huge* breakthrough. Who knew?
"I didn't know Jason was your ex-boyfriend!" exclaims Ms. Angleton. "He didn't even say anything about dating someone that lived here. Is that why you've been giving me dirty looks?"
"Yes, I thought you knew and was just rubbing it in my face. I mean, I'm done with him, but it still sucks," says Ms. Dozier.

"Look, I didn't know anything about that, and Jason and I aren't even together anymore. I don't have any problems with you and don't want some guy that was in my life for all of ten minutes," says Ms. Angleton sarcastically, "to cause a problem where I live."

I look at both women, and I am already feeling relieved by this realization as it may just fix itself.
"It sounds like this was all a miscommunication," I say.
Ms. Dozier looks from me to Ms. Angleton and says, "Look, I like it here and don't want any problems either. I won't give any dirty looks. And, Susie, Sarah doesn't have parties and didn't park in my space. I apologize for lying. I was just feeling jealous and angry. I just want to forget about all this."

I could tell Ms. Angleton agreed, but I wanted to ensure I still held them accountable for their actions. "Today," I say, "I'm not going to issue any lease violations. However, if either of you have any future incidents, I will have no other choice than to issue a violation that will go in your file."

Ms. Dozier nodded her head and stated, "I completely understand. Are we done?"

I nodded yes as Ms. Dozier rose from her seat and walked back to her apartment.

Ms. Angleton sighed and smiled at me. "Thank you, Susie, for listening to me. I told you that she was harassing me, and although I tried to blow it off, I truly appreciate you listening to what I wasn't saying and acting on it. If it wasn't for this meeting, this whole thing could have been worse, so thank you."

I smiled at Ms. Angleton and thanked her for her attendance and walked her out of the office. Although it wasn't the worst situation I've dealt with, it was sticky and challenged me to not only listen with my ears, but to recognize the body language and facial expressions I received. Sometimes listening doesn't pertain to just that moment in time. It is listening over a span of time and really paying attention to those smaller details that will assist you in heading in the right direction. People want to be heard—whether it's through what they are saying or how they carry themselves—and it's our job to truly listen to what they are saying.

Problem solving is a helmet that is utilized every day; whether it's with an employee, resident, or family member, there is always a degree of problem solving. The question is, How do you handle a problem, and what are the steps to solving it? In case you didn't already know, there are over fifty different techniques to problem solving, and each one equally valid. The question is which do you use naturally, and what is most effective? With this in mind, I'd like to share with you an experience I've had in problem solving.

A couple of months after the Ms. Dozier and Ms. Angleton saga, I noticed that my team was showing signs of distress. Debbie (leasing professional) was calling in sick more often, Sandra (leasing professional) was coming in ten minutes late at least twice a week, and Lynn (assistant manager) was walking around with a scowl on her face. Not the best environment to have for a successful leasing day. My outside team was not in the best shape either. Robert (lead maintenance) was out on medical leave, so that left Andy and Colby (assistant maintenance) temporarily in charge of scheduling and ordering supplies and ensuring Lisa (porter/housekeeper) was on schedule with her unit turns. Both were stressed and lacked communication, which created anxiety and disorganization with the team. I definitely had my work cut out for me.

It was Monday morning and the sun was shining bright, making everything glow. It was a hot summer, and I was thankful for the small breeze that shook the leaves on the trees slightly. When it's unbearably hot, we typically see an increase in negative activity. Why? Not sure, maybe the heat makes people crazy and impatient. Just an assumption. I walked into the office a bit earlier than usual to give myself a head start in preparing and hopefully steal a few minutes to catch up on a few pending items. I begin wiping on the tables and organizing the chairs when Lynn walks in. She announces a greeting as she walks to her office to place her purse down. She comes out a minute later to grab the duster and begins dusting the blinds as she opens them. I can tell something's wrong, but I make small talk to hopefully shake the mood she's in.

After a few minutes, she sighs loudly and says, "Debbie is really getting on my nerves lately. She's always forgetting the small details on her applications, and I can't get her to move someone in on the computer to save my life. Sandra's also come to me to complain about how she won't open the models and leaves it up to me every day. It's not fair that she's able to decide what she will and will not do when we are all supposed to be chipping in. Sorry for dumping on you all at once, but I'm just so frustrated I can't hold it in anymore."

I paused for a moment before speaking. "Lynn, I didn't realize this was becoming such a problem for you. I'll talk to Debbie and Sandra and see if we can work it out."

Lynn replies, "I don't think Debbie is going to listen. She never does, and I can't see her improving. If I were you, I would fire her." This was obviously more than just a little frustration.

I say, "I can't fire someone without giving them an opportunity to improve. She probably doesn't even know what she is doing wrong. We have to communicate that to her first and then support her as she corrects her performance."

Lynn doesn't look convinced and states, "I guess. I hope you're right because she is causing major problems with everybody."

At that, she turned to continue opening the blinds and brushing the duster over them. I continue wiping the tabletops and organizing the furniture until the clubroom is good as new. A few moments later, Sandra arrives and greets Lynn and me before jumping on balloons and preparing her sparkle bucket to open the models. Everyone worked quietly but diligently to prepare the office with few words of small talk.

Later that afternoon, I called Sandra into my office to discuss the frustrations Lynn had mentioned. "Sandra," I start, "how are things going in your opinion with the organization of duties and overall office atmosphere?"

Sandra looks at me a bit perplexed and says, "Why? I didn't do anything, did I? I think everything is fine."

"You didn't do anything wrong. I was just checking in with you to see how things are going and if everything is OK," I said.

Sandra takes a deep breath and says, "Since you brought it up, I am uncomfortable lately. Lynn and Debbie have been fighting and are always talking to me about each other. It's uncomfortable for me, and sadly enough, I can see each one of their points. I feel like they are just picking on each other."

I thought about this for a moment, and I have been concerned with how much Debbie has been out sick, and now the conversation with Lynn. What Sandra was now saying did make sense.

"I don't want you to be uncomfortable, Sandra. If you were feeling this way, please feel free to come and talk to me. I want you to be happy when you come to work," I say with a big smile. "You can't lease a home if you're not happy."

She smiled and thanked me for listening and went back to work.

Since I'd talked to the office team and had somewhat of an idea of what was happening, I decided it would be best to continue to investigate and call in the maintenance team to get their take on how things were going. I called Andy and asked him to take a break from his makeready for a moment to meet with me. A few minutes later, he comes in and states, "Yes, ma'am, you wanted to meet with me."

I asked him to have a seat and stated, "Yes, Andy, thank you for taking a few minutes to meet with me. I wanted to check in with you and see how you are doing." I left it at that and waited a moment while he contemplated my question for a few seconds.

He responds, "I didn't want to say anything, but since you asked, I'm really tired and frustrated. Ever since Robert's been out, it's just been Colby and me running everything, and Colby is too slow. He always wants to look at everything before I order or before I hand out the schedule like he's my boss. If he wanted to look at it, he should have helped me do some of it. He tells you that he's helping, but he doesn't do anything."

"Have you talked with him about it?" I asked Andy.
Andy stated, "No, he won't listen. He just wants to do whatever he feels like. I can't wait for Robert to come back."
"I'll talk to Colby about this and see if we can come to a mutual understanding," I reply.
Andy states, "OK. Everything else is fine, just a ton of work to do."

"Well, I won't take any more of your time, thank you."
With that, Andy thanked me and went back to work. I called Colby and Lisa next, and each one of them had similar frustrations with Andy and each other. My last call of the day was to Debbie. I called to check on her well-being and to see if we could expect for her to work as scheduled. She too had many areas of concern with both Lynn and Sandra, and as suspected, the stress was now affecting her health, and she was just not motivated to come to work.

That night, I sat and thought about the different conversations I had with each employee and looked for common threads of complaints. I also evaluated each situation separately to attempt to work through possible solutions; however, one thought kept coming back to me. No one is happy in their workplace. Not one employee had a positive comment to make, yet they all continued to work as diligently as they had before. As any leader would when coming to this realization, I looked within to determine if there was something I could have done to create this environment or if I needed to change my habits and visibility with my team. There are always areas of improvement, and each one of us could be better to those around us, but how do I create this type of environment in a positive way? Suddenly it came to me: an idea that may assist in changing the environment in a positive way.

The next morning I had a new pep in my step, a new glide in my stride. I had a plan, and I was ready to share it. I called the entire team into the clubroom, locked the front door, and set the return time for an hour later. I had stopped on my way in and bought coffee, orange juice, and breakfast tacos for the team to enjoy as we conducted our meeting. Tacos were always a great way to bring a smile to someone's face. They all came in and grabbed their breakfast and took their seats, and I anxiously waited until they were all comfortable.

"Good morning, everyone," I began. "Hope you had a good night's sleep and are enjoying the breakfast. I wanted to take a few moments this morning about a few items and how we can enjoy our jobs again. Yesterday, I had the opportunity to speak with each one of you about the progress we are making as a team and how you were feeling. To my surprise, most of you indicated a discomfort in your working environment and expressed dissatisfaction with a coworker's contribution to the team. There were some overlying items that all of us can improve on such as communication. We need to take our time when communicating and ensure that we are providing each other with all information needed to be effective in our job. It takes the entire team doing their part to be successful, so everyone has to pitch in and talk to one another if you see an area of improvement. If you can't seem to get along, come see me, and we can all talk together to find the solution needed to get us all on the same page.

"The second item is simple displeasure and frustration over small mistakes or incidents that are occurring. We are all human, and although we should always strive for perfection, we should not expect perfection—otherwise, we are setting ourselves up for disappointment. I challenge you, as individuals, to think about what you could have done differently to avoid a problem, and I can almost guarantee you that you'll see the problem a bit differently. At the end of it all, I also see a tendency for all of us to focus on the negative or what someone is doing wrong instead of recognizing the areas of success or thoughtfulness."

The entire team listened intently, and I saw a few slight nods, which instantly gave me a bit of relief. *With their listening, this may work.*

I continued, "In the spirit of turning our negative environment into a positive environment, we are going to start a new program called Good Deeds. We will have a box at the front of the office with a sign as you enter announcing this program that prospects and employees will participate in. The rules are simple: we will observe and write down positive acts that our coworkers are doing. For example, if I see Sandra see Ms. Garza struggling to get out of the car and run out there to assist her, I would write that act down with Sandra's name and place it in the box. Or if I see Robert taking initiative and assisting Lisa with grounds, I may write that act down and place it in the box. At the end of the month, we will pull the acts and sit down together to go through them. The person with the most "acts" documented will receive an Employee of the Month status—which will include their picture posted at the front, a gift card for dinner, and a movie for two."

The team looked at each other with smiles and began nodding. I could feel the excitement and was already seeing a change in their attitude. The problem wasn't solved, but we made a great first step that the entire team agreed to.

Over the next few weeks, the team seemed happier, and "acts" were flying into the box by the flock. Debbie was present every day since our meeting, Lynn was smiling again, and Colby and Andy seemed to be working better together and came to me when they couldn't come to an agreement. There were still arguments here and there, but the arguments didn't become attitudes, which kept everyone moving in a forward direction. I decided it was time to talk to each individual again and check their feeling of the work environment now.

First was Lynn. I pulled her aside and asked her how she was doing. She couldn't have been more pleased. Apparently, Debbie had come to her the day after our meeting and told her she had trouble remembering the process she needed to take when moving someone in. Lynn took the time out to walk through it with her, and now Debbie was taking care of the move-ins without any further issues. In fact, Debbie and Lynn had become so close that Lynn was working with Debbie on other areas of training simply as a resource for Debbie in succession planning.

Next was Sandra. Sandra was nervous from the beginning but seemed to have forgotten all about the Debbie and Lynn drama. She was just as happy as could be and didn't have any complaints. Third was Debbie. Debbie was equally complimenting of both Sandra and Lynn and was even sharing the responsibilities more and admitted to being lazy and realized how much work she was putting on the other two. She too was enjoying her time with her team. I called in Andy, Colby, and Lisa and received more of the same feedback. The problem had been solved.

At the end of it all, it wasn't just the problems themselves but the attitude the entire team was exhibiting. The workplace environment was negative; therefore, the staff was negative and began picking on each other. After implementing a program that forced them to see each other in a positive light and recognize those positive acts, it changed their overall view of the job and had a positive feel for their work environment. I was incredibly excited that the problem had been solved, and we were a better team for it.

The Hat of Patience—Customer Service
Dawn Daffinee, CPM®

Working at a variety of properties has provided me with experiences that are irreplaceable but couldn't have helped me with what was to come.

It all started with an invitation for a property supervisor position in New Jersey. The offer was sent by a midsized banking company headquartered out of Florida to manage their portfolio in New Jersey and New York. It was a huge leap for me and my family, but it truly was a great opportunity, and I quickly accepted the offer. I had approximately three weeks to pack all my belongings, prepare my son and daughter for the trip, and settle all my affairs. The first week of preparation was brutal. The moving company couldn't meet my deadline, the car needed a new tire, and the kids are hungry all the time. It was definitely a "Calgon" kind of day. The second week was much easier to handle, and I was now working on the fun stuff like searching for a place to live (which was number one on my list), setting up my accounts, and finalizing my new job's paperwork. I was so excited to begin my journey and couldn't wait to enjoy the new city with my family.

Two days later, I was on my way. I found the perfect condo located near Ocean City where the boardwalk was only a few minutes away. When we finally arrived in front of the condo, I stopped and stared at what was officially my home. It was a short stack building with large windows facing the street and a common front door that was secured for what looked like twenty-four hours a day. It was an older building with chipping gray paint but the kind that added character. There was a small stoop leading up to the front door with a series of names and buttons to the left. There was a code pad in the middle, and I punched in the code the landlord had provided me over the phone. I walked into a large hallway with doors on each side and small numbers indicating the number for each condo. Our condo was on the third floor, and I walked up a long staircase covered in red and gold carpet framed by a scratched-up oak banister. *This was going to be great for moving in furniture*, I thought to myself. Once I arrived at the condo, I was pleased with the layout and loved the view. I was right; this was going to be *great*!

The following Monday, I received my assigned portfolio and couldn't wait to get out to each one and get to know the teams and the tenants. The first building was a class-A office building in downtown Newark. The building stood twenty floors high and was covered in glass. The entry to the building had tall dark green pines framing the front door and an electronic board greeting you as you walked in. The floors were covered in a swirled cream-and-brown marble floor with small silver and gold carpets in each elevator corridor. Each floor was customized to the tenants' specifications, so depending on the floor you visited, you would either walk into a similar-styled marble floor and glass doors or rich dark mahogany floors with large mahogany framing around the walls. The building housed primarily doctors, so keeping a clean and fully functional building operating efficiently was essential.

The second building was the House of Music building in East Orange. The House of Music was a local venue where acts like Kool & the Gang had played. It had a green facade with swirly orange lines forming into musical notes. Inside the building was a small seating area surrounding a dance floor and a stage where the acts would perform. There were also several music reels in the back room that looked as if they had been there for years. My first order of business was to order a dumpster and hire a contractor to clean it out.

In addition to the two buildings, I also had a shopping center in Stanton Island, New York, in my portfolio. It was a decent enough project but was under receivership. This meant the owner was unable to make the mortgage payment, and the bank hired our management company to manage the property. There were definitely some challenges, with the largest and most obvious problem being the trash. The trash was overflowing and seemed to be a fairly frequent problem, considering the amount of trash around the enclosure. I made note of the problem and labeled it as a priority to take care of immediately.

I made it a point to drive out to the shopping center once a week and quickly realized that the pickups were not happening regularly, which was what was causing such a horrible mess by the Dumpster. I first checked to make sure the invoice to the trash company was being paid, which it was. Next, I called the trash company to see if I could obtain a copy of my contract and let them know what my concern was. The representative I spoke to was very quick to rush me off the phone that I was sure I wasn't going to get my hands on the contract or better service. I decided that I would seek out additional vendors to bid the job. As I began researching vendors to contact, one of my tenants—Debbie, from Stanton Island—called.

"Hi, Debbie. How can I help you today?" I said.

"I think you need to take a look at what you're doing before you make any changes," Debbie said in a matter-of-fact voice.

"Excuse me? What are you referring to?" I said, truly confused.

"I'm talking about the work you're doing to change the trash company," Debbie stated.

"Oh, I'm sorry if I sound taken aback, but why are you concerned about the trash vendor we decide to use?" I said curiously.

Debbie sighed deeply over the phone and, in a cryptic, tone stated, "The property is *controlled*." Immediately after, Debbie hung up. That was weird. Why would a tenant call to stop me from changing trash vendors? What does *controlled* mean?

I stopped calling trash vendors and placed the project aside for now. There was something strange going on, and I needed to find out what. I contacted a few of the other tenants with nothing in particular, but it allowed me to make small talk and see if there was anyone else that was concerned. Nothing. I wasn't sure where to go with it from here, so I decided to hang it up for the night.

A couple of days later, I decided to call Debbie and find out what exactly she meant by our earlier conversation. I called a couple of times but couldn't reach her, so I decided to pay her a visit. When I arrived, I was in luck; she was there.

"Hi, Debbie," I said casually.

Debbie looked up and grinned widely. "Hi, Dawn, good to see you."

"Do you have a moment to talk?" I asked patiently.

"Sure, let me just wrap this up. If you'll wait for me in my office, I'll be right there."

I nodded and walked to the back office where I sat in a small chair facing a "too large for this space" desk. Behind the desk was a small credenza covered in binders.

Debbie walked in shortly after and quickly shut her door. "I'm glad you came. I was wondering if you were going to come in and talk to me. I could tell you had no idea what I was saying but couldn't explain over the phone," she said in a rapid pace as she searches the room.

I was taken aback by her (what looked like) enthusiasm. "Well, I'm glad I came in today. Can you tell me what you meant by a 'controlled' property?" I said.

"A 'controlled' property means that the property is 'controlled' by the mafia," Debbie said in a whispering voice.

You have got to me kidding me, I thought to myself.

Debbie could tell she shocked me but proceeded on. "When the property was still cash flowing, the owner paid a small 'fee' to maintain the business. I'm not sure what he got back in return, but I do know he was paying a pretty large chunk of money every week.

I sure would hate to be in that situation. Anyway, since the property is now in receivership and owned by the bank, the mafia no longer gets their money. Unfortunately, the trash removal company is also owned by the mafia, which is why the place looks like it does." Debbie stopped and just stared at me, waiting for a reaction. I had a choice. I could either freak out (which is exactly what I felt), or I could thank Debbie for her time and freak out in the car. I chose option B as you could imagine.

I got to my car and panicked for what felt like hours, but it was really only ten minutes. I gathered my thoughts and decided I would find a way to fix this. However, I would not be fixing this today. What I needed was a glass of wine and a mind-numbing TV show with the family to absorb and conquer tomorrow. So that's exactly what I did.

The next day, I was reenergized and ready to conquer the world. I decided that I would tackle the mafia first and all other matters later. I also decided that in order for me to make any headway, I was going to need to approach this situation as I would with any other vendor. I had to forget about the possible ties to the mafia and just push forward.

I contacted the trash removal company again and received the same type of response as the first time; however, this time, I stopped the representative from talking and asked for the manager. The woman on the other end immediately placed me on hold. Once again, time felt like dripping honey, slow and persistent. Finally, someone picked up on the other end and said, "This is Fred. How can I help you?"

"Hi, Fred. My name is Dawn, and I'm calling in regard to the Suns Shopping Center," I said nervously. "I'm calling in regard to the lack of trash removal at the property," I continued.
There was a long moment of silence.
"Yeah, what about it?" said Fred.
Oh gosh, this was not working out like I'd hoped.

"Well, Fred, I am the new property supervisor," I said, emphasizing the word *new*. "And the trash out at the property is just out of control, and I could really use your help to schedule regular pickups."
Another long pause.
"We'll tell you when we can pick up the trash. You pay and then we will pick it up. Capisce?"

Yikes!

"I understand, Fred, but I checked our payment history, and it looks like we've paid on time. Is there a payment missing I'm unaware of?" I said nervously, knowing I was now pushing my luck.

"Hold on," said Fred abruptly.

Another long and excruciating wait until the representative came back on the phone.

"Hi, ma'am. Fred asked me to finalize the call and let you know that the crew will be there on Wednesday."

I was shocked. It had actually worked; I had won the small battle and had my service restored. The rest of the day was all gravy from there. I was so afraid to push too hard, but in the end, handling the situation as I would any other vendor and providing a level of customer service while doing it really worked out for me. It was definitely going to be a great job!

The Helmet of Customer Service—Too Much?
Kelly Blaskowsky, CPM®

C ustomer service is a primary requirement when you work in the real estate industry and is grilled into you as you move up the ranks within the real estate field. Well, I say . . . Can you provide too much?

It was a cloudy afternoon, and I was working for my second week in a 140-unit community. The property was small but had plenty of character. The landscaping was filled with mature trees and a small courtyard area with a colorful plastic play set. Near the playground were picnic tables set near a finely charred community BBQ pit. Nothing fancy, but it did get the job done and was appreciated by all that lived here.

The clubroom area was split into two buildings joined by a cement-covered breezeway. On the left-hand side was the clubroom, which was available to rent by the residents should they want to have a small party or gathering. The room contained a sofa and loveseat situated around a large wooden coffee table. The coffee table had a variety of magazines, which covered the dings and scratches in the wooden coffee table. Coasters were in the middle; however, it was clear they were for direction more than they were for protection of the table.

Off to the left sat a small kitchen, fully equipped with a fully functional stove, refrigerator, and small dishwasher. There were water bottles in the fridge along with what looked like two bagged lunches. To the right was a small 32-inch TV and a small hallway that led to the bathroom. Overall, it was cute and cozy and just enough room to have a small gathering.

Across from the clubroom was another door that led directly into the management office. The property was older, and I could certainly tell by the look and smell of the tiny office. As you walk in, the door pushes a small bell to notify those in the back office that company has arrived. In the front sat a single desk with a few papers on top and your typical penholder and stapler. Over to the side of the desk sat a small table with additional magazines and two 1980s-style desk chairs and a small penholder in the middle. The pens were wrapped in green plant tape and had a large plastic flower on top. Cute idea, but it left the smell of plant wax on your hand once you used it.

Toward the back of the office was a small desk against the wall with a small 19-inch monitor (and not the flat-screen kind) and small printer on the side. Behind the small desk was a larger desk piled with files and papers along with several office supplies and a rolled-up piece of foil from a previously eaten lunch. There was also a small closet located next to a large lateral filing cabinet and a large makeready board (otherwise known as a whiteboard to track apartment turnover). The closet contained all the supplies needed and a key box that held all the apartment keys to the community.

It was my second week working at Shady Grove, and I absolutely loved it. My manager was a tall blonde woman that looked older than she was due to her chain-smoking and personal habits. She was training me to one day become a manager because she was moving on to a larger property that required her specific skill set. I was more than happy to learn as much as I could from her. She definitely knew the property and seemed as if she knew every resident and their families by first name. It was amazing watching her.

There was one resident in particular that would come in every day around 4:00 p.m. without fail. He arrived back from wherever he went during the day around 4:00 p.m. and was dropped off by a local transportation company. The resident's name was Bill, and he stood approximately six feet tall with stark white hair and dark sunglasses.

He had a long black cane that never left his side, and he always seemed so eager to come to the office. Once he arrived, my manager would come out to greet him and say, "Hi, Bill. Ready for your magazine?" Bill would smile and nod.

I'm sure you've guessed by now that Bill is blind. Not the kind that needs glasses but 100 % blind, and every day he came in to have a magazine read to him. My manager would grab him by the arm and lead him into the clubroom area to begin their reading session. They would stay in the clubroom for about thirty minutes before Bill headed back to his apartment. My manager would come in and go back to her desk as if coming back from a small detour. I loved how dedicated my manager was and how she always took time out to make someone feel good. I admired her for it and vowed at that moment to follow in her footsteps and make sure Bill continued to have his magazine time.

The time had finally come, and my manager was no longer going to be reporting to Shady Grove. It was now up to me to keep the property going and ensure business continued as usual. I was nervous but excited. I followed my notes to the letter to ensure I had all my duties completed and kept my eye on the clock. I was patiently waiting for 4:00 p.m. when Bill arrived so I could talk to him and let him know I would now be reading to him.

Finally, the time came, and I was ready. Magazine in hand, I stepped out into the breezeway and watched as Bill's small bus pulled up to the front of the property. I waited and watched as each passenger exited the bus with help from the bus driver. As the last person exited the bus, I realized that Bill was not coming. Disappointed but not defeated, I went back into my office and set the magazine back on the table. *"He must be sick,"* I told myself. It wasn't that I needed him to come in, but I wanted to fulfill my vow and was fairly anxious to make the transition.

The next day got a bit easier, and I felt fairly comfortable with the schedule I was building for myself. I came in a little early to clean up the office and make sure we were ready for business. I walked the common areas, fitness center, business center, and clubroom to make sure they smelt good (as well as it could, considering the age) and was sparkling clean. Sometimes you can't help the age of the inventory or building, but you are in complete control of the cleanliness, so making sure the property and common areas were clean was always a priority for me.

Once everything was ready for business, I sat at my desk to begin my report for my boss. I had only been working for about thirty minutes when I heard the small gold bell ring above the front door. I immediately stood from my desk and walked to the front with a smile on my face, ready to greet today's first customer. To my surprise, there stood Bill.

"Hi, Bill," I said with as much enthusiasm as I could to hide my surprise.
"Hi, where's the manager? I need to speak with her," he stated with his lips drawn into a straight line.
"She's been moved to another property, but I'm more than happy to help you," I said with a smile. I knew he couldn't see my smile but hoped he could hear it in my voice.

"No, you can't help me," Bill stated as he walked out of the office and waited for the small bus to pull up. Funny, I had always noticed his arrival but really hadn't noticed his departure. I guess getting to know him and reading to him wasn't going to be as easy as I thought.
I turned and went back to my work. The day went as most days do—fast and furious. Four o'clock came and went and no Bill once again.

The next couple of days were the same: come in to open up, clean the common areas, walk my property, and begin on my deliverables. People came in and out either to lease apartments or just to see what the apartments looked like. I didn't mind; I loved showing off the property and pointing out its best attributes. It was easy to sell something you loved. I loved the property so much that my family and I decided to move in, which made my commute incredibly easy and lunches at home a great source of savings for us. Living on the property helped me to see and notice all the smaller details that needed to be addressed. Some would see it as a burden since you're technically working all the time, but I saw it as a luxury. Living and experiencing life on the property I was managing was quite exhilarating. Life was good, but I was still slightly bummed that I could not keep the same customer service the previous manager had provided.

A few months later, Bill walked in and stood in the doorway. "Good morning, Bill. Haven't seen you in a while," I said in as friendly a way as possible.

Bill stood still for a moment and sighed. "OK, I guess I'm ready for you to read to me."

I was shocked for a moment and had nearly forgotten about magazine time.

"Sure, Bill. I can certainly do that for you. What time would you like to go through the magazine?"

Bill was quiet for a moment as he pondered my question and said, "I'm not sure. I guess whenever my bus gets here."

"That sounds great," I said with a smile on my face. "I'll see you then."

Bill left, and I turned to head back to my office. *What a weird encounter that was*, I thought to myself. However, I quickly shrugged it off and kept working. The morning went by quickly, and before I knew it, I looked up and it was 4:00 p.m. Bill's bus had just pulled up, and I saw Bill exit the bus. I quickly grabbed a magazine off the table and walked out into the breezeway. "Hi, Bill. Ready for your magazine?" I asked.

Bill shook his head, and I took his arm, leading him into the clubroom. I walked Bill over to the couch, and he slowly lowered himself to the couch cushion. He adjusted slightly and said, "Go ahead, I'm listening."

I suddenly felt very strange. Where do I start? Do I read every page? Oh, how I wished I had asked more questions about magazine time. Guess I was going to wing it. I opened the magazine and began reading the table of contents and asked Bill which article interested him, to which he replied, "Don't you have any new magazines?"

I said, "Umm . . . Let me check."

I shuffled through the magazines and very quickly realized that they were all outdated. I never noticed anyone updating the selection, but apparently, Bill did.

"Shannon always had updated magazines for me. I knew you weren't as good as Shannon." And with that, Bill stood and slowly made his way to the door.

I sat there shocked and feeling defeated. My one shot to make this right, and I blew it. I know what you're thinking: "Why was this so important to me?" Well, it wasn't necessarily an "important" task, but when I accepted the property, I was really hoping to keep the things that I felt were important. Magazine time was important since I knew Bill had very little friends, and I hated to see him so disappointed over the previous manager's departure. Sure, there were plenty of residents that had noticed my efforts and took the time to thank me, but having even one resident upset really bothered me. Once again, I was determined to make this right.

The next day, I brought in three brand-new magazines I purchased from the local grocery store. I set them out on the table and threw out the older magazines. I set up as I typically did and started my day. As usual, the morning went by quickly and 4:00 p.m. came quicker than I thought. I still had quite a bit to do before I could leave for the day and was almost hopeful Bill would go straight home today as he had previously. The small gold bell rang out, and I stood and walked to the front door. There stood Bill, patiently waiting for my arrival.

"Good afternoon, Bill. I have some new magazines for us today," I said.
"I'm ready," Bill stated.
I was beginning to see that Bill was a man of few words. I took Bill's arm and led him into the clubroom. We sat on the couch, and I began reading the table of contents again. Bill stayed quiet but attentive. He

nodded at the subjects that were of interest, and I flipped to the page to read the article. After thirty minutes, I began to wrap up the last article. Once I finished, I stood and walked Bill to the door.

He shook my hand and said, "Thank you for reading to me. I'll see you tomorrow." Bill turned and began slowly walking to his apartment as he tapped the sidewalk to ensure there were no obstacles in his way. I turned to enter my office and grinned a large Cheshire grin. *Finally, I won over the resident and could resume what the previous manager had started,* I thought. What a great feeling! I went home with a sense of accomplishment and felt good for helping someone.

The next few days were all a blur, but I continued to take thirty minutes out of my workday to provide magazine time to Bill. He was slowly becoming more comfortable and began to spark small talk. He asked several questions about me, my family, and basic work questions.

I was open to his questions as I felt he really just needed a friend, someone to talk to. However, some of my peers who knew about Bill thought I was crazy to spend so much time with one resident, but I felt compelled to do so since he really didn't have anyone to talk to. Day after day went by, and the cost of the magazines was beginning to become a burden on my own pocketbook. I also noticed that what used to be a thirty-minute session was now taking forty-five minutes to an hour.

I was definitely getting sucked in too far with Bill and was beginning to take more time and money than what I had initially intended. One day, Bill came in as always and eagerly awaited my reading. I sat in front of Bill and sighed. "Bill, I cannot afford to continue to buy magazines every day. What do you say we meet once a week instead?" I asked, slightly hesitant and worried about his response.

"No worries," Bill said to my surprise. "I have my own magazine today."

With that, Bill pulled out what appeared to be a book but was, in fact, a magazine. I smiled and began reading. We passed our thirty-minute mark and were well into an hour of reading.

"Bill, let's wrap it up for today, and we can continue tomorrow," I said, exhausted and ready to get back to work. Bill nodded and rose to exit the room.

He stood at the door for a minute and stated, "It's OK. I'll come at 6:00 p.m. tomorrow so you won't have to worry about going back to work." With that, he walked out of the clubroom and back to his apartment.

OK, I thought, *this might be good. If he comes later in the day, then I can get my work done. How bad can it be?*
Don't you wish you could take your words back even if it was in thought only? Well, I definitely did.

The next few days, Bill came in at 6:00 p.m. and would keep me reading for a solid hour. I wasn't getting home until 7:00 p.m. every day. I was all about helping and providing a service, but this was taking time away from my family, from my kids. Was this right? I had to fix it. I had to find a way to control what seemed to be such a great idea at first. I had to tell Bill. I had to be honest and let him know that I could no longer allocate so much of my time to reading and would have to go back to the thirty minutes we had before.

But how do I do that when I know he doesn't have anyone else? My mind and my heart were not seeing eye to eye. Was what I doing crossing the line, or was it truly providing great customer service? I thought long and hard about it and finally came to a conclusion. I was going to talk to Bill tomorrow and get this whole thing under control. It wasn't wrong to want to allocate time appropriately; I just had to frame the discussion in a way Bill could understand.

The next day, I was tense but ready to have a talk with Bill. The morning crawled by as I anxiously stared at the clock, daring it to move faster. At long last, 4:00 p.m. came, and I thought I would catch Bill at the bus. To my disappointment, Bill was not on the bus. I went back to work and buried myself in spreadsheets and graphs. I nearly forgot the time when the small gold bell rang as the front door was opened. I looked at my clock, and it was exactly 6:00 p.m. *Bill*, I thought as I stood, preparing myself for what felt like a very uncomfortable conversation.

"Hi, Bill," I stated with a half-smile.
"Hi, I'm ready, and I have a new magazine for today," Bill stated as he held up a thin magazine.
"Great, thank you for bringing the reading material. Bill, I hate to do this, but I really need to change our time back to 4:00 p.m. and limit our reading to the thirty minutes we started. I'm so sorry, but I can't continue to stay at work so late. My family needs me too, and I want to get home in time to make dinner."

Silence filled the room as Bill grinned with a look of no concern.
"Sure, we can change the time back," said Bill. "I thought this worked better for you, but we can make this our last night. In fact, I'd like you to read to me at your apartment. I heard you lived here, and this way, you can still see your family."

bar

He seemed so sure this was a great idea, and me being so new to my job and filled with guilt for his lack of friends, I said, "Sure, that sounds like a good idea."
So not a good idea . . . If only I knew what I know now.

I stood from the couch and grabbed Bill's arm to lead him out of the apartment. I announced to my family I would be back and begin to slowly walk Bill to his apartment home two buildings away. Bill thanked me for the night and told me how much he appreciated me taking the time out to read to him. At that point, all the frustration and anxiety I was feeling earlier melted away as I realized this night had made him feel special. I felt good about what I had done and began to feel a sense of relief that maybe he wasn't taking advantage but really didn't know how to handle himself.

We arrived at his front door, and Bill took his keys out of his pocket and asked me to open the door. I unlocked the door and looked in a dark and gloomy apartment home. The chairs were faced toward the walls, and there wasn't a TV in sight. I know he can't watch TV, but it seemed strange not to have one, even if it was just for the noise. I walked Bill into the apartment and said, "Well, thanks again for a great night and see you tomorrow."

"Wait," Bill said in an urgent manner. "I need one more favor. Can you please clean out my cat's litter box?"
Wow, I couldn't believe it. Was he really asking me to clean out his cat's poop? I didn't even like cats. What do I do now? Walk out and say no? Tell him I can't clean out poop because it will make me puke? Once again, I found myself in a bad position, all because I tried to be nice and provide good customer service. Was this too much? Had I led myself to this place? I knew one thing for sure. I was stuck cleaning poop, and I would not ever be allowed to be placed in this position again.

I said OK but was now angry. Angry that I was cleaning up what was technically a stranger's cat poop, angry that I allowed this to get out of hand, and even angrier for not drawing the lines when I still had the power to do so. I was sure the previous manager hadn't cleaned poop in the name of "customer service." I finished the job and quickly said good-bye and exited the apartment home before I could be given any other chores to complete.

That night, I thought about the events that had occurred and my determination to win over one resident out of 140 that were on property. Why did I feel so compelled to win this one resident over? It was my inexperience in thinking that everything the previous manager had done had to be replicated and kept. Looking back, I realize that I could have provided the service to retain the resident without allowing anyone to cross the line into my personal life. It was only one night, but it was more than I wanted or would allow again.

Bill was just fine with the thirty minutes I allowed him, but I found out the hard way that I needed to control that relationship and not allow my desire to provide the best service to cloud my judgment on where to draw the line with residents. We work in a place that provides homes for people to live and raise their families, and although we are managing the property, we do not need to become friends to provide the best service. Most people are more than happy with a friendly smile and attention to their needs. Customer service should always be a focus point of our business, but it should not cross over into your personal time.